What This Book Will Do for You

If you deserve a raise or promotion, this book will help you to make a strong case for getting it. Before you are through, you will be well prepared and ready to manage any objections your boss might throw at you. You will have the tactics of a well-defined strategy with which to work, and you will make a clear and self-confident presentation that will make it hard for your boss to say no. So read on . . .

Other Titles in the Successful Office Skills Series

Get Organized! How to Control Your Life Through Self-Management

How to Be a Successful Manager

How to Read Financial Statements

How to Write Easily and Effectively

Increasing Your Memory Power

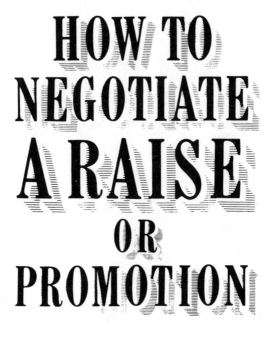

HOW TO NEGOTIATE A RAISE OR PROMOTION

Donald H. Weiss

amacom

American Management Association

Library of Congress Cataloging-in-Publication Data

Weiss, Donald H., 1936-
    How to negotiate a raise or promotion.

    (The Successful office skills series)
    Includes index.
    1. Promotions. 2. Wages. 3. Negotiation in business.
I. Title. II. Series.
HF5549.5.P7W45   1986   650.1'4   85-26746
ISBN 0-8144-7643-0

Printing number

10 9 8 7 6 5 4 3

CONTENTS

Introduction—How to Get What You Deserve   1

1. **How to Command a Raise or Promotion**   3

    Believe in Yourself   4

2. **Timing Is the Key—When to Ask for a Raise or Promotion**   5

    How a Union Contract Can Affect Your Request   6
    The Impact of Standardized Systems for
       Determining Pay   7
    Checking Out Labor-Market Conditions   8
    Checking Out Market Factors   10
    Checking Out Your Organization's Financial
       Position   13
    The Best Time to Make Your Move   13

3. **The Art of Negotiating—How to Get What You Are Worth**   15

    Planning   17
    Goal Setting   18
    The Critical-Incident File   20

4. **How a Win-Win Strategy Will Succeed with Your Boss**   29

    The Win-Win Strategy   30
    How the Win-Win Strategy Works   31
    Techniques for Effective Negotiating   34

5. **Getting Your Boss to Agree—Resolving Any Disagreements and Reaching a Consensus**   38

    Haggling—The Fine Tradition of the Marketplace   43

6. **Additional Points About Asking for a Promotion**   44

    Factors to Consider in Planning Your Career   44

7. **Now Is the Time for You to Act!**   46

    Decide on Your Goal   47
    Select Your Strategy   47
    Negotiate Effectively   48

Index   51

About the Author   53

Introduction—How to Get What You Deserve

Everybody who works for a living—and that means most of us—*knows* that their pay doesn't match their worth. Just ask and you'll hear, "This company would stop, drop dead in its tracks if I walked out. Yet you'd never know it if you could see my pay check."

At the same time, when you ask such employees why they don't walk in and ask the boss for a raise or promotion, you conjure up in their minds the image of Dagwood Bumstead spending the whole day psyching himself up to barge into Mr. Dithers's office, only to get a kick in the pants for his effort.

Or how about this one? Dagwood, determined to get that raise, stands in front of a mirror, shouting out loud every negative response he expects to hear from Mr. Dithers. After listening to the imaginary Mr. Dithers putting him down time and again, Dagwood bursts into the boss's office and yells at the startled old fellow, "You can keep your raise, you skin-flint."

Sure, you've seen those comic strips and thousands like them. On the other hand, when was the last time *you* asked for a raise or promotion? And—especially since you're probably not getting what you think you're worth—why haven't you? Isn't it high time you stopped playing Dagwood and got with the program?

It took Charlie Goode five years to get with it. Five years had gone by since he was promoted to head bookkeeper for a produce distributor in Dallas, and he hadn't received a raise once in all that time. The firm gave him a payroll and insurance clerk, a billing clerk, and an accounts receivable clerk. It even gave him stock in the company. But a raise? In real cash?

"From those tightwads I work for?" Charlie grumbled when his wife asked him, yet again, if he had requested a raise. "From those penny-pinchers?"

"You've worked for them 12 years, 5 as head bookkeeper. You're entitled."

"You'd think they'd have more consideration."

"That's what I'm saying," Flora snapped.

Charlie glared at his wife—angry at the situation, not at her, but wishing she wouldn't go on about it. "You're right. Twelve years, and I get even less consideration than those scruffy loaders on the dock." His anger intensified; his resolve strengthened—for what seemed to Flora to be the thousandth time. "Well, time's come to do something about it."

Flora sighed. "Yes, dear." She had heard it all before. Well, maybe not a thousand times, but often enough for her to say, not unkindly, "Time's come to do something about it every few months for the last three years. Each time, you leave here all fired up. Then you get stuck in that traffic on Central Expressway and come down with a case of the chickens by the time you reach the office. How's this time going to be different?"

"You'll see. You'll see."

In fact, this time *will* be different. Mr. Charlie Goode—head bookkeeper for a family-owned produce company in Dallas—will ask for his raise. And those "tightwads," those "penny-pinchers," as Charlie calls them, will give him that raise. Because this time, Mr. Charlie Goode will step out of the role of Dagwood Bumstead and into the role of effective negotiator—a role that until now he didn't know that he, too, could play.

What's the difference? This book. It will take Charlie, and you, on a journey through the mysterious world of negotiating—world in which preparation, planning, and presentation conquer the nervous fears of the Dagwood Bumstead in us all.

Come along with Charlie and learn how important it is to believe in yourself, to believe in your power to get what you want. Learn how to decide when to ask for your salary adjustment or for that next rung up the ladder. Learn how to prepare by deciding on a strategy for negotiating and by marshaling and documenting all the relevant facts. Learn how to ask for a private place for the meeting and for enough time to reach a conclusion, or at least to reach a point at which little remains to be said or done before a decision can be made.

Learn how to state your case calmly and unambiguously, asking for agreement at each step before moving on to another point. Learn also how to show your boss the benefit to the company of giving you that raise or promotion. Learn how to bargain.

Chapter 1

How to Command a Raise or Promotion

That's *command*, not *demand*. Dagwood sleeps on the job, he's almost always late to work, he misses deadlines, he packs his lunch in his briefcase and leaves the Biggs account at home. Usually, Dagwood messes up. Yet he *demands* a raise fairly regularly. Not too smart. Maybe Mr. Dithers is right to kick him in the pants.

Now Charlie Goode. That's a different story. He's earned the right to ask for a raise. Only he doesn't really seem to believe it. Or if he does believe it, he doesn't believe in himself or in his right to ask for that raise. He doesn't accept his own power.

Believe in Yourself

We all have a need for personal power. Whether we're talking about meeting physical needs or safety needs, social needs or ego needs, or the need to fulfill ourselves, we want to feel as if we're really in control. The trouble is, few of us feel that way. Many people experience a huge sense of futility, believing that destiny and other people grasp their lives tightly in an iron fist.

Those who feel dominated by others accept whatever they can get, no matter how hard they've worked for their organization. Bob Cratchit, in Dickens's *A Christmas Carol*, comes to mind as a good illustration of the set-upon, hardworking clerk whose ungrateful employer has to undergo a miraculous conversion before he'll grant the poor man a reasonable salary. Bob can't take the credit for his increase in pay. No. Sometimes humility and charity toward others ill-befit the person whose family depends on his or her earnings.

The more powerless among us usually bring their sense of futility upon themselves, either by not acknowledging their need for personal power or by not exercising it when they have the chance. Obviously, to be successful in asking for what you want, you have to believe in your right to do so. You may not know yet whether you've earned it (that comes later), but unless you believe in that right, no ghosts of whatever kind will terrify your boss into handing you an unasked-for raise.

Socioeconomic conditions may hold you back. No question about it. Racism, sexism, ageism, depression, recession—many factors can impact on you just when you think you have the power to do what you want with your life. The conditions of the labor market, the general market conditions of your industry or related industries, and the financial condition of your company itself will all play a role in your ability to get what you want (and I'll discuss them in more detail later). Still, if you never ask for what you want, you'll have no chance to get it.

Okay, so believe in yourself. That's a place to start. Believe that you're capable and competent, that you've made a contribution to the organization that merits a reward, that your absence would affect the company adversely. If *you* don't believe those things, no one else will.

Take stock of yourself. You're worth more than you get, and you know it. You've accepted the responsibility of your position and a whole lot more. You're not just demanding a raise or a promotion; *you've earned it*—and you've got the documentation to back you up.

What now remains for you to do is to build your case to prove that you believe correctly. Unless you do, you'll persuade no one to agree.

To be persuasive, you'll need good timing, excellent preparation, a good presentation, and some carefully practiced negotiating skills. Let's take a look at timing first, because choosing the right time will help. Choosing the wrong time will only reaffirm the feeling that destiny and other people control your life.

Chapter 2

Timing Is the Key—When to Ask for a Raise or Promotion

Timing is not merely a matter of time. It's a matter of the nature of your organization. It's a matter of market conditions. It's a matter of the conditions that affect the organization as a whole. Do you want that raise or promotion? Even if you've earned it, unless you consider those factors, you can count on having your negotiations blow up in your face. If nothing else, your familiarity with the relevant factors will put you in a position where your boss can't argue you out of your request with inaccurate information or a distorted picture of how things are.

Charlie's confident now. He knows where he stands, but let *him* tell it. Let's go back to the breakfast conversation with Flora.

Flora: What's so different this time?

Charlie: First of all, I know where I stand. I know just how this company works. I know what's in the budget and what's not. I know what's going on in the marketplace, too. What other bookkeepers are making. And I know just how well this company is doing. This time, Flora, I've done my homework, and I'm ready.

Flora: What's all that going to do for you if they say no?

Charlie: It's going to be hard for Adam to say no to me— not with record I've run up. And I've got the data to prove it.

Flora: Well, I've got to admit you sound different this time.

Charlie: I *am* different. I've got the right on my side, and I'm going for it.

When the right is on your side, why *not* go for it? To get the right on your side, though, you need to gather the data Charlie told Flora about. You have to dig a little. If it's worth it to go for it, it's worth it to go for it with all you've got.

When considering the nature of the organization, give thought to whether or not it's bound by a union contract— especially if you happen to be a member of the union. Consider also whether it uses an employee-classification system—for example, the Hay system—for raises and/or promotions or whether it uses a fixed cost-of-living-adjustment plan or some other relatively inflexible way of rewarding employees. The reasons for taking this into account should be plain.

How a Union Contract Can Affect Your Request

Unlike a standardized system of salary adjustment, union contracts leave little room for individual negotiation. Wages determined by union contracts are, by their very nature, fixed through collective bargaining. If you belong to that union, by asking for a raise on your own, you risk having management laugh at you and having the union steward let you in on the facts of life—in no uncertain terms.

On the other hand, if you feel you're being paid less than scale or that you're not receiving bonuses or benefits you deserve as spelled out in the contract, you can and should ask for what you feel is coming to you. Just go through your steward to do it. Prepare your own case—even present your own case—in the way I'll suggest, but make sure your union rep's there.

Even if you're not a member of a union under contract where you work, that contract may still affect you. Some companies tie all wages and salaries to the contract. That sometimes works to your advantage, especially if you can show that you're earning less than for comparable union jobs. It sometimes works to your disadvantage if policy dictates that no one receives more than union scale and you believe you deserve more. Check it out. It's an important aspect of your planning.

The Impact of Standardized Systems for Determining Pay

On the other hand, a standardized system, such as the Hay system mentioned earlier, leaves more room for bargaining. Though most of these systems use precise mathematical calculations, too technical to describe in detail, they all classify people into specific job categories, grade levels, and pay standards within each class of work.

Almost all of these systems then divide the pay grades in each category into subgrades—ranging from a minimum in the grade to the maximum. Most people entering a new pay grade start somewhere between the minimum and the midpoint. If, when entering a new position, the pay offered is not to your liking, the system leaves open the door for negotiating an entry point.

The system leaves open the door, but how about company policy? If it, too, leaves open the door, have at it. If not,

7

you've got some hard choices to make. If company policy closes the door on negotiating your position and you believe the system's treating you unfairly, you may have to decide whether it's worth it to you to stick around or whether you should look for somewhere else to plead your case.

The merit system some organizations use gives you the right to negotiate the level of pay grade to which you believe you're entitled. Not many people governed by such a system exercise that right, and just because your company uses a merit system, it doesn't follow that the company recognizes your right to bargain at review time. Still, no one can blame you for trying, right?

Checking Out Labor-Market Conditions

Now, Charlie works for a company in which neither union contracts nor a standardized system exists. Come to think of it, Labor Department studies show that only 20 percent of all American workers are covered by union contracts, and only a relatively small number of medium-sized companies use a standardized system (though most large companies do). Small-sized companies, such as the one for which Charlie works (and for which most of us work), give little, if any, thought to developing a detailed compensation plan for their employees. At Charlie's office, it's every man (or woman) for himself (or herself). It always has been that way.

Most small- to medium-sized firms are like that. They decide on wage scales and benefits based on what the owners or managers think they can afford as well as on what they think is fair—or on what they believe the employees are willing to accept. The law of supply and demand of labor plays a larger role in those decisions than does the minimum-wage law or other provisions of the Fair Labor Standards Act.

In this type of company, the question of when to ask for a raise or promotion has less to do with the nature of the organization than it does with timing. If your situation is in fact ruled by the law of supply and demand of labor, picking a time when vast numbers of people who do your type of work and share your skill level are responding to every ad may lead to disaster. For example, right now (spring 1985), roughly 200 people answer each ad for a training specialist with three to five years' experience—and many of the résumés list five to ten years' experience. You need to check out the labor-market situation in your field before you take any rash action.

Studying your market conditions requires only that you read your own trade journals, local newspapers, and national magazines (such as *Business Week, Newsweek, Time, Inc.*). You can find the Labor Department statistics in most public libraries. Talk to employment specialists, such as your state's employment service or reputable headhunters. Check out what's happening.

Check Out Labor-Market Conditions

1. What is the supply of experienced people in your line of work?
2. What is the demand for those people?
3. Into what industries will your skills enable you to transfer should you not get the raise or promotion you think you deserve?
4. What's the demand for your skills in those industries?
5. If you have to do it, what's the best way of going about searching for another job without jeopardizing the one you have?

If the supply is low, if the demand exceeds the supply, if your skills are transferable to industries with a higher demand than supply, and if other opportunities are available, you should consider the possibility of asking for a raise or promotion.

No one will argue against asking for a raise or promotion when the labor supply is lowest—when the fear of losing you to a competitor becomes your ally. Yet no one expects you to wait until then to meet your own needs. You might wait as long as Charlie did. Still, giving due consideration to other labor-market factors and conditions affecting the organization as a whole could make a significant difference in whether or not this is the time to make your request. Check things out in the same places and at the same time you check out your labor-market conditions.

Charlie Goode has learned that bookkeepers in different industries receive different wages, even during the same time period. In one—say, High Tech—a head bookkeeper might be making $33,000. Charlie's earning only $30,000 in a produce company of the same size as some High Tech firms. So let's borrow the idea of "comparable worth" from the jargon of Equal Employment Opportunity (EEO), as it applies to women and other groups protected by the law. I'll stretch the concept to cross over between industries.

What's the difference between doing the work of head bookkeeper in a produce-distribution company and in a High Tech firm? You maintain the books in either one—regardless of the products or services of the company. The contracts and contract administration may differ, but bookkeeping is bookkeeping. Therefore, if you think you can make a case for it, you decide that the timing is right to ask for a raise when you think that the *high end* of the head bookkeeper's pay range is to your liking, whatever the industry in which it appears.

At the same time, don't forget what I said about the law of supply and demand. It, too, will affect salary ranges. When labor exceeds demand by any significant amount, it depresses salaries. A glut of head bookkeepers on the market will therefore work against you. Timing—it's everything.

Checking Out Market Factors

When you should ask for a raise or promotion also depends on the conditions that have an impact on your organization as a whole: the market factors affecting your industry, the financial condition of your organization, or the rate of growth of either (or both).

If you work in Houston, in an oil field–related industry, now (spring 1985) is not the time to ask for anything. In the last two years, one major energy-products producer has reduced

----

Check Out Market Conditions

1. What is the demand for your organization's good and/or services?
2. Has that market stabilized, or is it growing or shrinking?
3. How are prices moving in your industry—up or down?
4. How are the market shares in your industry being divided; what is your organization's share of that market; and is that share growing or shrinking?

If demand is high, if the market is growing, if prices are moving up (but slowly), if the market shares of your industry are fairly evenly divided, or if your organization has a very large share of the market and that share is growing—then, all other things being equal, this may be a good time to request your raise or promotion.

----

its workforce by 72.7 percent (from 1,100 in 1983 to 300 today). That's typical of that industry these days. The same holds true in such industries as semiconductors, steel, and other metals. Last year was the time to ask for a raise or promotion in the automobile and automobile-related industries. If the Japanese do flood the market again, this year will not be the year to make your case. It's quite likely that your otherwise mild-mannered and pleasant boss will turn into a raging Mr. Dithers if you do.

Of course, some companies weather the storms of their industries. (Here's where being able to read financial statements comes in handy.) Several oil and gasoline producers in Houston are not only alive but doing quite well. While many airlines are laying off personnel, still others are hiring. Market conditions *alone* shouldn't dictate when you ask for what you want. The financial condition of your own firm has to be considered also. If your firm is doing O.K., then it *may* be O.K. to ask.

Only "*may* be O.K." because sales volume, the ratio of sales to buyers' inventories, and profit margins all factor in.

Here's a tip: Learn to keep your eye on how the buyers of

your products use their inventories. If your company's sales increase while your buyers' inventories decrease or at least remain stable, then conditions seem right for asking, because the sales increases are as a result of real inventory turnover. Your goods are being used up, and the sales outlook appears strong—that is, if the cost of production and/or sales in your firm hasn't been escalating at the same time. That'll kill the company's profit margin.

Everyone has to watch that profit margin. That's an especially important barometer in service-oriented companies, which have no buyer inventories to measure. When profits are down, managers balk at granting raises, even though sales volume may be up. If profits (as opposed to gross sales) are increasing, you *might* want to go for it.

But if you work in a product-oriented industry, keep your eye on sales versus buyers' inventories, as mentioned earlier. If the size of your buyers' inventories increases at the same rate as your sales or faster, beware. Your buyers are stockpiling—hedging against inflation or against diminished supplies. They will soon stop buying, and your sales and profits will plummet. Just ask anyone in the semiconductor industry what that means for your chances to get what you deserve.

Not too many people in those companies ask for raises or promotions these days, because in 1984 microchip users went on a buying spree but few producers noticed that they were hoarding the chips. Not until the third quarter of the year did they begin using up inventories—and stop buying. They're still not buying, and the producers are drying up. Only the strongest will survive the present shakeout.

That's why you have to consider the growth potential of your industry's market and/or that of your company. Markets disappear, especially in consumer goods. Video-game manufacturers can tell you about that.

Some companies grow too fast, too soon, and the law of diminishing returns cuts the ground out from under them. (Tne law of diminishing returns says that as you increase any specific resource, especially labor, the return on investment in each addition is less than it was on earlier units of that resource.) Hiring new people may not necessarily profit a company. New hires can have the effect of cutting into profits, and whether or not a raise will be granted will have little to do with the fact that you've earned it.

Most of this information is available to you, by the way, in the same places where you find information on your labor market.

Checking Out Your Organization's Financial Position

The information about your company's financial picture may not be as readily available, especially in privately held firms such as Charlie's. Still, you can find out some of it by asking discreet and tactful questions of the person who holds a position comparable to Charlie's. As head bookkeeper, he has an enviable vantage point.

- -

Check Out the Organization's Financial Position

If you were an investor, would you buy stock in your organization? Here are some important questions you need to answer:

1. How much were gross sales during the last 12 months? Are they growing or shrinking?
2. What are the organization's total assets—that is, how much could the company get if it sold off everything it owns?
3. After all expenses have been subtracted from the company's gross income, what was its net income over the last 12 months? Has net income been growing or shrinking?
4. What is the organization's total debt—that is, how much does it owe to creditors and lenders—and could the value of the assets cover the debt if the company had to sell off part of those assets?
5. How much would the company owe to its stockholders if it had to sell off everything or buy back its shares?

6. How much of your company's net income comes (1) from sales less cost of operations and (2) from the sale of stock or from ways of raising money other than through sales?

If the percentage of indebtedness is small, and if the net income is high as a percentage of sales but low as a percentage of owner's equity, your organization's in pretty good shape. All other things being equal, go for it.

The Best Time to Make Your Move

When is the *best* time to ask for a raise or promotion?

Make your move when the majority of the aforementioned factors turn favorable—when the company's success makes it impossible to refuse your request.

We all know, however, that the *best* time may never come. In that case, *you need to pick the time when,* given the conditions, *making the request has a fighting chance and when you can demonstrate that you contribute to the company in some significant way—that the company would be less than it is without you.*

Chapter 3

The Art of Negotiating—How to Get What You Are Worth

Once you believe in your own power and have determined that the time's right, you're ready to start. No, don't go marching straight off into the boss's office and say, "I deserve a raise." Not yet. You have a long way to go before you're ready for that.

One reason many people don't get the raise they want is that they don't know how to ask for it. They ask for a raise, not for a specific salary figure. When they're turned down, they go off and sulk, or get angry, or quit, or do something equally ineffective for making their lot better. They don't realize that they must be prepared to *negotiate* for what they want if they're to get anything at all.

When people think of negotiating, they think of governmental action or labor-management relations. It's something the secretary of state or the president does. It's the job of diplomats. Union leaders negotiate contracts. Workers merely ratify them. The average person, it seems, never negotiates.

Not true. People negotiate all the time—with friends and relatives. They discuss (sometimes they argue about) what movie to see, where to go on vacation, where to live, what to eat, what to wear. The success of a marriage depends on the partners' ability to negotiate. Given that so few people know how to negotiate, no wonder that the divorce rate is as high as it is!

What am I talking about? It's simple.

Negotiations take place when two or more people have to reach an agreement in principle, or when they have to choose between alternatives, or when they have to take a specific action.

When you see it spelled out that way, you can see just how often you do negotiate for what you want.

What makes it seem as if people don't negotiate very much is that they usually do it without consciously realizing that that's what they're doing. That's because most negotiations go on without conflict. Though all negotiations begin with a felt need or a sensed or recognized problem, most give and take goes on peaceably and amicably. Conflict arises when you and/or the other people involved think that successfully negotiating something means *winning*.

Then you become fearful and/or frustrated. Since negotiating is the process of agreeing on something together, if someone who is a party to these negotiations wants the whole cheese for himself or herself, then you're into competition, not negotiation; and competition, uncontrolled, breeds conflict. At best, competition, especially if unexpected, threatens people's self-esteem and need for personal power. The negotiations then turn into a test of wills, a struggle for control. When someone takes an all-or-nothing-at-all posture, the other party tends to meet force with force, and "the ignorant armies clash by night."

Sometimes you become hostile during negotiations because your economic or physical well-being is on the line. That's exactly the case when negotiating for a raise. The possibility of being turned down drives Dagwood into telling Mr. Dithers to keep his darned old raise. You become fearful. You put the proverbial chip on your shoulder and lose the battle before you begin to fight.

That also happens when you're not sure of the outcome you want, when it's as ambiguous to you as it is to the other party. That's why it's important to ask for a specific amount of money rather than to ask simply for a raise. You become hostile toward the other person because it seems as if he or she is being deliberately obtuse and dense. Without this book, Charlie might have burst into the owners' offices and, after knocking things about for a half hour, probably blurted out: "You know darn well what I want. I want a raise." But then again, so does everyone else.

One last source of conflict comes from not knowing how to bargain. It's related to wanting all or nothing at all. Fixing in your mind one and only one acceptable percentage or sum of money leaves you with no room to maneuver. You get turned down, and you're thwarted. The refusal blocks the outcome you want. That frustrates you, and you come out swinging. No, Charlie, that's not what I mean by the art of negotiations.

An effective negotiator has a well-formulated plan based on a rational strategy, and he or she knows what to ask for, how to ask for it, and how to make the case persuasively enough to get it.

Planning

Charlie's ready this time. He's armed to the teeth with facts—labor conditions, market conditions, the financial condition of the company. He knows where he stands now, that's for sure.

But hold on, Charlie. Those facts only buttress your *resolve*. You still have to plan (1) an overall strategy, (2) the case for your raise, (3) your bargaining chips, and (4) how to manage objections. Through careful planning and rehearsal, you'll minimize anxiety and prevent the frustration that comes from not anticipating possible obstacles.

In other forms of negotiation, the first planning step consists of identifying the issues. Just what problems are there to be resolved? Unlike in those other forms of negotiation, the issue here is clear—Charlie wants a raise. Still, he should consider these questions before embarking on his mission:

1. How long has it been since I received a raise or promotion?
2. Have I truly earned my raise or promotion, or am I asking out of need or want?
3. How successful have others been recently in getting what they've asked for?
4. How receptive was the boss, or did the others have to work hard for what they got?
5. What did they do right or wrong (depending on the outcome they had)?
6. Do the benefits outweigh the risks?

Once you've answered those questions to your satisfaction, and assuming you still believe that the time is right and that you deserve to have your request honored, then you have to set your goals.

Goal Setting

In negotiating a raise or promotion, as in any other form of negotiation, you have to know what you want as your outcome. You have to set a realistic goal for yourself. Unless you know what you want, chances are you'll wind up with far less than would make you happy (if you get anything at all).

In any form of negotiation, it's best at this early stage of planning to keep your goals and objectives flexible. What do you think would happen if Charlie asked for a 16.75 percent raise and would accept nothing less? That would bring his salary up to $35,000 a year. He had better prepare himself for the rude shock of his boss's laughing at him.

Any goal, to be well formulated, must have a target, but the target must be realistic and achievable if you are to hit it.

A realistic goal is one that everyone would agree fits with conditions. Charlie's ideal may be 16.75 percent, but how often do you hear of someone's getting that large a raise all at once (other than in professional sports)? That percentage would bring Charlie $2,000 over the top end of the range for bookkeepers. Then again, even though that's kind of high, it *is* something to consider.

But unless Charlie asks for it, he'll have no chance to get it. Who knows? Maybe his boss would grant that high a raise. Stranger things have happened.

Still, you have to ask whether that goal is something Charlie could really hope to achieve. Given the conditions of the company and the marketplaces he's studied, maybe the goal is somewhere within the realm of reason, but the decision belongs to someone else. He might not be as enthusiastic as Charlie about "all things being equal." That goal may in fact be out of reach at this time.

A more realistic, achievable approach would be to answer three more questions:

1. What is the minimum I am willing to accept?
2. What is the maximum I can hope for?
3. What can I realistically expect from my boss?

You answer the first question by weighing all the facts of your personal financial situation. What amount of money would improve your financial situation enough for you to feel good about yourself and your position? Pencil-and-paper computations would include monthly payments, small investments, new purchases of necessities you lack, and so on. These calculations help you maintain your objectivity. They help keep your feet on the ground and control any possible irrational greed. Let's say that, in Charlie's case, 6 percent will cover the increases in cost of living and other expenses that have accrued over the last five years. That should bring him up to the same level as other people who got somewhat smaller raises each of the last five years.

As for the maximum you can hope for, I'm still talking about keeping the goal setting realistic and achievable. Yet you'd want to set the goal high enough in order to have room in which to retreat (and I'll explain that business of retreating in a moment). That 16.75 percent goal may be a figure for which Charlie can shoot as a maximum. He has nothing to lose by asking. Since the going *top* salary for his position and amount of experience is $33,000, why not ask for something over that figure? As I said, if he doesn't ask for it, he'll never get it, and the boss might just say, "Sure."

Well, if getting the maximum raise is unlikely, and the minimum would be just barely satisfactory, then it's important to be ready to settle on something in between. For Charlie, that would be somewhere between 6 percent and 16.75 percent. Perhaps 10 percent. That would bring him to the same level as the highest-paid head bookkeeper at this time.

How realistic or achievable would that in-between point be? That's where all the data collection you've done pays off. If you have a solid base of facts with which to debate, you increase your chances of coming off with the raise you can realistically expect—but only if you document your case that you have earned your raise.

The Critical-Incident File

If you're like Charlie, you probably work for a company that doesn't have a formal performance-appraisal system. Even many very large companies don't have one.

And if the organization doesn't have a formal appraisal system, chances are it doesn't have either a formal personnel manual or written job descriptions. With neither a performance-appraisal system nor a personnel manual nor written job descriptions, chances are also good that no one has kept a record of anything.

So how do you document that you have in fact earned your raise or promotion?

Organizations that mandate a periodic performance appraisal usually also mandate that supervisors keep a file of events for each employee. This is called a critical-incident file—a record of good performance as well as poor performance. (*Critical* in this instance means *important*.) But how many people keep their own record to complement the supervisor's?

Again, like Charlie, you probably take each day as it comes, letting events flow by without regard to how you record those events, if you record them at all. Few people ever keep a diary of their workday, even those who keep a personal diary at home.

And more important, where no system exists, who keeps any records at all? If you do, you're the exception, not the rule.

First, I'll show you a way to reconstruct the past in order to support your case for a raise. Then, I'll show you how to produce a critical-incident file that you can keep from this point forward.

Without a formal personnel manual, your organization has no prescribed procedures, either for granting raises or for you to ask for a raise. That could work to your advantage. Whether or not you get that raise will be strictly between you and your boss. Therefore, you have to be better prepared than he or she when you sit down across the bargaining table from each other.

Preparing a description of what you do on your job provides you with a starting place. Typically, a job description spells out the duties the organization expects anyone in your position to perform—a list of daily, weekly, or periodic activities. You do them or you don't do them—typically. But the mere fact that you follow the prescribed list and that you perform those duties won't really help you get your raise or promotion.

That's because that list consists of the *minimum* requirements of the job. To command what you deserve, you have to show that you've *exceeded* the minimum requirements.

Nothing impresses a manager (and I include owners in that category, too) as much as bottom-line results. Old-fashioned managers used to say, "And what did you do for me today?"

You're going to show your boss what you did for him or her today, yesterday, and every day since your last raise or promotion by (1) developing a results-oriented job description and (2) writing a résumé that emphasizes achievements rather than tasks.

If your boss expects you to do something for him or her, just what is it that you are expected to do? What results does your boss expect you to achieve on a daily, weekly, or periodic basis? What goals has he or she expected you to accomplish that contribute to the overall goal or mission of the organization?

Make money. That's what most people mean by "bottom-line results." When they talk about their organization's overall mission, they usually refer to making a profit by offering goods or services to a given marketplace.

So you make a contribution to that mission if you personally produce or, assuming you're a manager, if the department you manage produces income or reduce(s) the costs of doing business. You make a significant contribution when what you produced has had an important impact on the company's ability to achieve its overall goal.

Most people don't make money for their companies. Sales and marketing people actually make the money, and unless you're in either of those departments, you're just like most other employees. You spend money. You have to spend money to make it, it's true, but most of us have to show how we helped that bottom line by *not* spending money that won't produce money in return.

Let's say, as in Charlie's case, that you're the manager of a department that spends money—in salaries, wages, benefits, equipment, supplies, physical facilities. You operate a cost center, as distinguished from a profit center. The conclusion is too obvious. If you're the manager, what does your boss expect?

That's right. He or she expects you to operate your cost center at the lowest possible cost for the highest possible return on each dollar spent in that cost center. He or she expects you to make effective use of all the resources at your disposal—to get the maximum output from the organization's investment.

O.K. Now you have a goal, or at least a standard on which the merits of your case can be based. Let's use Charlie's job to illustrate how to put together a results-oriented job description. His goal is shown in the accompanying sidebar.

When Charlie has to reach his goal is stated as, "During the fiscal year . . ." How about *your* time frames? Do your company and department operate on an ordinary calendar-

---

Charlie's Goal

During the fiscal year, oversee the financial-records department of the company and operate within a total budget of $XXX,XXX.XX by

1. Supervising the activities of the bookkeeping staff.
2. Generating cash-flow statements.
3. Producing trial balances for the accountants to audit and to use for reporting to the company's management.
4. Paying all bills.
5. Depositing all income.
6. Collecting overdue accounts.
7. Reviewing and recommending cost-saving measures.

---

year basis, or is your work judged on a periodic basis, or does no one give any thought to how long it takes you to achieve your results?

On a blank sheet of paper, try out this idea: "During the time since my last raise (or since I was hired, or since I was promoted) . . ." Then, follow it with your target.

You can use Charlie's goal statement as a model for how to write your own target. The required target at which Charlie has to shoot is "to oversee the financial-records department of the company and operate within a total budget of $XXX,XXX.XX."

What's *your* target? Whether or not you're a manager of some kind, state what you think the company or your boss expects from you. Write out both the time frame and your target.

Each part of a goal statement answers a question. The time line answers the question of "when" or "by when" or "during when." The target answers the question of "what." Now, in Charlie's goal statement, what's that list that follows the word *by* called?

Those are the objectives he has to accomplish in order to reach his goal. It's a list of broadly stated steps he needs to take in order to achieve the results expected of him. The list of objectives answers the question of "how"—but only partially.

Let's take two of those steps and look at them a little closer before you write a list of your own. First, we'll look at "supervising the activities of the bookkeeping staff," and then we'll look at "reviewing and recommending cost-saving measures."

"Supervising the activities of the bookkeeping staff" gives only a broad guideline. The next question is, "How does Charlie supervise the activities of his bookkeeping staff?" What activities does he have to perform to accomplish this objective? By golly, we've finally reached the list of daily, weekly, and periodic duties with which most people usually start when they analyze their jobs.

1. Assign work to each person in accordance with his or her job description.

2. Review each person's work to check for errors.
3. Monitor each person's attendance and punctuality.
4. See to it that each person completes his or her assignments on time.

The list can go on, obviously, but I don't think you need more detail in this area. Later these *minimum* requirements will be used to show how much more Charlie has done to contribute to the profitability of the company.

The last item in the list of Charlie's objectives speaks directly to the issue of contributing to the company's profitability. The company has mandated that he "review and recommend cost-saving measures." What follows is a list of activities that would help him accomplish this objective.

1. Request and receive from all department managers suggestions for reducing costs in their areas.
2. Examine the suggestions with the managers to test their feasibility and actual profitability.
3. Recommend those measures that withstand their tests.
4. Find ways to increase the turnaround time between delivery and receipt of payment.
5. Find the least expensive methods for collecting unpaid bills.

That's enough for that list. As you can see, for Charlie to answer the question "How do I achieve my goal," he has to divide the answer into two parts—(1) his broad objectives and (2) the specific, detailed activities he performs under the heading of each of the objectives.

This is called a results-oriented job description because the second list tells *what* Charlie does every day, every week, and so on, while the first list tells what *results* he achieves by doing those things. Together, the lists tell *how* Charlie achieves his broad goal of overseeing the department within his budget constraints. You can break down your job into those same two lists.

Take another piece of paper. Read the target you wrote for yourself earlier. Now answer the question "How did I reach that target during the time frame since my last raise (or since I was hired or promoted)?" Write one list of broadly stated outcomes or results you accomplished. Then, for each stated outcome or result, list the daily, weekly, and periodic things you did to achieve that particular result. Use Charlie's lists as models.

If you have trouble developing the broad objectives of your job first, try this. Make a list of every individual activity you can recall doing. Make it as extensive as you can. Then, group together all those things that seem related to one another. Separate those things out from other groups of activities. Finally, ask yourself this question:

Why did I do those things—that is, how did they contribute to reaching my target?

That will give you your list of objectives or desired outcomes for your job. On the other hand, if you can't see why you did those things, either you've been doing unnecessary work or you don't really understand the nature of your position itself. It'll be hard to ask for a raise or promotion under those circumstances.

Now, you may not be able to reduce all your activities into groups that contribute to achieving your goals. For example, perhaps during the last year you were asked to serve on a task force to help evaluate the effectiveness of a piece of machinery used in another department and to search out a more effective piece of equipment. It really didn't have anything to do with your immediate job requirements, but the company needed your expertise on that committee.

That's one sort of thing I'm talking about. Another might be that you spent a lot of time this past year, during working hours, calling different stores in order to comparison-shop for appliances for your new home. That's right. You'd better include such activities in your list, too. They could be used to counter your argument, and you need to be prepared for them.

So another bit of analysis will help you put those things in order. Ask:

1. Do any activities stand isolated from other activities?
2. If so, why did I do them—that is, how did those activities contribute to the company's overall mission?

If what you did made no contribution to the company's mission, you've been wasting your time and the company's time. You should cut it out, even if your boss required you to do it (such as running his or her personal errands). In such a case, you could point out how ineffectively your boss is using your time and skills. It's costing him or her money—money that could be used to give you your much-deserved raise.

If what you did does contribute, and if those activities are not directly related to the requirements of your job, then—especially if you were asked by management to do those things—you've got a strong piece of evidence in support of your case. *You've performed above and beyond the call of duty.*

When you've finished your analysis, return to your reading on this page. We still have to take Charlie's lists and look at *how well* he did his job. Remember that you won't command a raise just by meeting the minimum requirements. You need to find as many activities beyond the call of duty as you can.

Did you make your lists? Any surprises? Such as things you do that make no contribution either to your job's objectives or to the company's mission? Or are your tasks and your time well organized? If you've achieved your job's objectives, now you know why and how. If you haven't, you know that, too.

Let's see now if you really merit a raise. That can be done by examining Charlie's lists of objectives and activities and by drawing from them what I'll call his *résumé.*

In point of fact, it won't be a traditional résumé. It'll be a list of *major accomplishments* within Charlie's job description about which he's earned "braggin' rights" (as they say in Texas).

As supervisor of his bookkeeping staff, Charlie hired his employees. The effectiveness of his judgment is reflected by the fact that (1) he's had no turnover in five years and (2) his employees' attendance and punctuality are better than that of any other employees in the company. (If his firm had any work standards, he could compare their attendance and punctuality with those standards as well.) That has saved the company the costs associated with turnover and lost time.

Charlie's staff rarely make errors that reach his desk. He can document that whatever errors they do make never leave his office. The accountants and management itself have never seen mistakes in any reports or records he has developed. They've even complimented him on his outstanding record. That saves the company time and money as well, especially since audits are extremely expensive.

The fact that Charlie has developed the reports and records he completes is another key accomplishment. When he took over his position, he found several records that unnecessarily overlapped. Those redundancies created a situation where reports were taking too long to complete and caused too much dissatisfaction among the people who had to read them. Charlie cleaned up the management control reports, eliminated the redundancies, and trimmed out unnecessary or irrelevant statistical data. Report writing has become easier and less time-consuming, and report reading has become less of a burden for the managers.

I could take each item in Charlie's lists and show some way in which he has made a contribution over and above the call of duty, but, as an illustration, that would be overkill. Instead, I want you to go through your own lists and identify any and all things you did that went beyond the basic requirements of the job or made a significant contribution to your department's objectives or your company's overall mission. If you can specify dates and the value in dollars saved or earned, that makes your case even stronger. Use this format to develop your résumé:

Objective:

Activities:

Major Achievements:

Include awards earned, special training received, the publishing of a job-related article—anything job-related for which you've received recognition or have brought recognition to the company. Why? Those things contribute to what the accountants call "intangible assets." An organization lives or dies on its reputation (which is why newspapers boast of the number of Pulitzer Prize winners on their staffs). Anything you do to enhance that reputation—the company owes you for that.

One last point before I leave the subject of preparation and move on to the action plan itself. Documentation. Memories are short. At best, they're selective. You're at a disadvantage if you have to say, "Boss, remember when I did such and so?" He or she could too easily say, "No. I don't recall that at all."

Besides, people are more inclined to believe what they read than what they hear. Anything in writing or in print that you can put in front of your boss will have a much greater impact than anything you can say. That's why, from this point forward, keeping a critical-incident file on yourself makes sense. You won't have to scramble around for documentation the next time you ask for a raise.

Now that you know what goes into a critical-incident file, it takes very little effort to create one. You need a results-oriented job description; a résumé; award notifications, citations, atta-boy or atta-girl memos, reports you've written, income you've produced or money you've saved—anything for which you have been (or should have been) commended. Third-party comments help, too. Anyone who commended you for something becomes an ally in your effort to get your raise or promotion.

Your boss may also be keeping a file—a record of bad marks. You need to be prepared for that, too. Anytime something not so good happens, record the event. That means, write a memo to yourself describing what happened and why or how it happened. No excuses, now. Produce a straightforward account—whether or not it was your fault. That's right. Write it down. You see, your memory is selective, too.

All this may seem like a great deal of work, and for some people this much preparation may be unnecessary. You need to know just how much firepower you'll require when you sit down at the bargaining table. To know that, you'll have to make the proper assessment of your organization's compensation policies and your boss's receptivity. That's the first step in your action plan.

Chapter 4

How a Win-Win Strategy Will Succeed with Your Boss

So by now you know what you need to know about all your market conditions. You know what outcome you'd like to have, what minimum amount you'd be willing to accept or what position you want, and what you can realistically expect to get out of your boss.

You have a critical-incident file with adequate documentation. Your argument in defense of your request consists of your results-oriented job description and your résumé.

Now you need a surefire strategy for presenting your case and persuading your boss that meeting your request for a raise or promotion is as much in his or her interest, and in the company's interest as it is in yours. The test of the strategy consists of whether or not you can demonstrate those benefits without threatening to leave—or, in effect, blackmailing the boss. Threats or blackmail usually backfire unless your boss can't understand that he or she leaves you no other recourse.

You know, everyone has needs. Your needs were discussed when I talked about deciding on the minimum amount you'd accept. Your boss has needs, too. You manage your boss when you identify those needs and address them with any proposition you have to make. Another look at Charlie's situation will help clarify what I'm talking about.

Charlie has known his boss, Adam, for 12 years. He's quite familiar with the man's hot buttons—both to move him in the direction in which Charlie wants him to go and to move him in the opposite direction. One thing Charlie's learned about Adam is that he wants people to think well of him, to see him as an intelligent, rational manager. He may be tightfisted, but that's because, in his mind, that's how you succeed in business. Appeal to Adam's need for recognition and avoid triggering his need to protect the vault—those are crucial features of Charlie's strategy.

Next, Charlie has to analyze how the company can benefit from giving him a raise. If the labor market is tight, Charlie can count on that condition to be his ally, but if he can't count on a tight labor market, he'll have to come up with something that will move the company toward its goals—while, in fact, increasing an important cost factor.

What follows is a part of the beginning of the conversation between Charlie and Adam. The pleasantries, the small talk, have taken place already. Charlie is cheerful and calm because he's prepared and knows his cause is as just as it is well documented. Look for how he sets up the conversation that follows. I'll review it with you at the end.

Charlie: Well, thanks for meeting with me, Adam. I know how valuable your time is, and as I said, I don't think this'll take even an hour.

Adam: I appreciate your consideration. You said, if I remember correctly, that you want to talk to me about your salary. I imagine you're asking for a raise.

Charlie: To come right to the point, you know I haven't had one in five years, and I'd like to talk about it—first, to find out what you think about my work as head bookkeeper and then to tell you what I think. That way, I believe we can work out any differences between us and come to a reasonable, fair, and just resolution. How does that sound to you?

The Win-Win Strategy

There are four things to note before I outline the whole process. First, Charlie acknowledged Adam's need related to time while simultaneously expressing his own appreciation for the chance to talk about his raise. Second, he set up an outcome for the meeting—a reasonable, fair, and just *raise*.

Third, the words *reasonable, fair, and just* appealed to Adam's need for recognition in those terms. They also made clear to him that this was not just a raid on the vault.

Finally, Charlie also programmed the way in which the meeting would proceed. "Tell me what you think about the work I've done. Then I'll tell you what I think. Finally, we'll work out any differences of opinion." His question, "How does that sound to you?" checks out if they have agreement on the protocol. If they don't, Charlie knows he's in for a tougher go than he had hoped for.

Reaching agreement constitutes the heart of the strategy I've been illustrating. I've borrowed the whole process from an approach to selling I call client-centered sales—a way to meet your needs (make the sale) by meeting the needs of the client. It's a win-win strategy of negotiation that consists of finding:

those points of agreement or those elements of common interest on which both parties can build in order for each to benefit from reaching a mutually satisfactory resolution.

(The alternatives to the win-win approach would be a win-lose strategy, in which only you meet your needs or only the other person meets his or her needs; or a lose-lose strategy, in which neither you nor the other person meets any needs.)

Five distinct steps characterize this process of negotiation:

1. Setting the stage
2. Hearing out the other person
3. Explaining yourself
4. Resolving disagreements
5. Reaching consensus

How the Win-Win Strategy Works

We've already seen how Charlie set the stage for the whole process. Next, he has to find out his boss's opinions. You can't hope to achieve agreement on anything until you know the other person's point of view. If you have to ask for a raise or promotion, chances are your boss hasn't told you what he or she thinks about your work—except, perhaps, to criticize it. You need to ask for that information. You can't negotiate unless you know the other person's position.

Don't be afraid to ask for it, either. If you've built your case solidly, you have no need to be afraid to ask. You and your boss probably will disagree on one or more points. That's to be expected, but the mere fact of a disagreement shouldn't spell doom for the mission as a whole. *To guarantee success, you need to deal with those disagreements, but using as a starting place the points on which you do agree.*

Once you've heard out your boss's viewpoint, it's time to express yours—but be sure you have, in fact, heard out his or her entire position. I'll kill two birds with one stone with the next piece of dialog—first, I'll dramatize Adam's point of view through Charlie's feedback of it, and second, I'll illustrate how to use what is called informational feedback to summarize what has been heard and check it out for completeness.

Charlie: So, if I've understood you, Adam, you don't have many complaints. You like the work I've done, but you think I could have more control over my staff than I do. You think I'm a bit too easy on them. Is that right?

Adam: That's the gist of it. When someone's too easy-going, employees don't respect him or her the way they should. But otherwise, as I said, you've done your job. Where does that leave us, Charlie?

Charlie: I'm pleased that you like my work. I agree that I've done my job, but before I answer your question, I'd like to make sure you've said everything you think is necessary or want to say. I'd rather not cut you off.

Adam: No. That's O.K. I've said everything that's on my mind.

Now that Charlie has effective negotiating skills going for him, he's become tenacious, hasn't he? He won't give up until he believes he has everything he needs. Assuming that Adam's telling the truth, Charlie can go on to explain where he agrees and where he disagrees.

Charlie: I'm glad you were candid with me. It helps clear the air. As I said, I think I've done my job, too. In fact, where I disagree is on two main points. First, I think I've done more than just my job. I think I've done my job very well—extremely well, actually. I also think that I'm not too easy on my people. Rather, I think I'm fair and understanding, and as a result, I get more respect than you think I do. If we can talk this through, I think I can show you how both the department and the company have benefited from my work and supervisory skill. How do you feel about talking it over?

Adam: [*Grimly and with a touch of annoyance*] I don't see that it'll do us all that much good.

Let's stop here and take a quick look at what you've just read.

Though Charlie's words may seem a bit stilted, it's only because most people don't usually talk that way. But what I'm saying is that you can probably get more mileage out of talking that way than by countering with the most common reaction—anger. "What do you mean, I'm too easy and don't have my people's respect? How dare you say that!"

Charlie states his points of disagreement simply and straightforwardly, with an economy of language and with cool self-control. This is not the place to lock horns. After all, since he just told the boss "I disagree," he'd better do two things: First, he'd better let the boss know that he thinks this disagreement and its resolution benefit the company. Second, he'd better find out how the boss feels about discussing the disagreement. As you saw, the boss was none too pleased. Let's see how Charlie handles that.

Charlie: You seem upset, a little peeved.

Adam: Upset? Well, maybe I am. I'm not used to having my opinions questioned. You have to admit, that's a pretty brash thing to do.

Charlie: You don't like to be questioned this way.

Adam: You're right. This is my company, you know. I can run it as I see fit.

Charlie: You don't think talking out our differences can *ever* help the company?

Adam: Well . . . no. It's not that it can't *ever* help the company, but . . . Charlie, you asked my opinion, and I gave it to you. Why can't we just leave it at that?

Charlie: I know I asked for your opinion, and I know you gave it to me. That I disagree is important to me because I think your opinion may be holding up my raise. That's why I'm bringing up these issues. Since I know you to be a fair man, I'd really like us to discuss our disagreements and resolve them. In both the short and the long run, I think settling this matter will help all three of us—you, me, and the company—by removing a sore spot for me, by clearing up some issues for you, and by improving the morale of a number of people in my department. I think I can back up what I've said and make my case. I'd like a shot at it. What do you say?

Adam: It seems really important to you, Charlie. I guess maybe I wasn't being fair. As for whether or not my opinion's what's held up your raise, I don't know. Frankly, I haven't given any thought to it. You've seemed contented enough as things were. Your people, too.

Charlie has already successfully negotiated a point of disagreement—whether or not to discuss their disagreement. His success followed from the fact that (1) he didn't get angry, (2) he let Adam fully express his annoyance, (3) he gently moved Adam from an apparently inflexible position, and (4) he stroked Adam's ego while stating how resolving their differences will contribute to their achieving both personal goals and company goals.

Techniques for Effective Negotiating

Charlie took control of this meeting from the start, while he set the stage. Then, when he could have lost that control, he reasserted it instead by not losing his temper and by using a technique called *mirroring*: acknowledging Adam's feelings, reflecting back the feelings he observed. Instead of ignoring or bypassing those feelings, Charlie addressed them with mirroring statements that drew attention to them and helped

Adam talk about them. Get those feelings out and get over them.

If feelings stay locked inside, they interfere with negotiations. You think one thing is happening when in fact the opposite may be occurring. You have to find out what's happening by watching and listening for cues that signal feelings—such as tone of voice, facial expressions, body posture. When you think you're observing some sign of feelings or emotions (whether for good or for ill), you have to take time out to discover whether your perception is correct.

Sometimes what you're experiencing doesn't make itself immediately clear. Then, you have to do something most people don't like to do or find difficult to attempt. You have to stop the flow of the conversation, diplomatically, and use a technique called *checking it out.*

For example, if Charlie hadn't been correct about Adam's being upset or peeved, he could then have said: "I think it's important to both of us to know just what you do feel, Adam. If you're not upset or peeved, yet I'm feeling something coming from you, I'd like to know what it is you're feeling about this." Charlie's checking out what's happening before getting caught up in the wrong interpretation of Adam's feelings.

At the proper moment, when Charlie saw Adam's attitude harden, he asked a key question that, though risky, forced his boss to reassess what he had been doing and saying. "You don't think talking out our differences can *ever* help the company?"

That question does much the same as a mirroring, but it focuses on what is said, on an opinion, or on a belief rather than on a feeling. It's a paraphrase rather than a mirroring statement. As a paraphrase, it gives informational feedback to the other person, and in this case, it makes what the other person said look a bit silly. That's why it's risky.

This paraphrase should be used sparingly and only when you believe it wouldn't back the other person into a corner from which he or she has no escape. It can be called *the reduction to absurdity,* and I had Charlie use it only because it would help Adam come back to his usually fair-minded behavior—or at least to his perception of himself as fair-minded.

Charlie acknowledges Adam's feelings (mirroring), and he also acknowledges what Adam says. He frequently uses informational feedback, but not always in the stilted form ("If I understand what you've said, you've said such and so"). Sometimes he uses it in a more conversational way ("I know I asked for your opinion, and I know you gave it to me").

Informational feedback lets the other person know that you're listening and that you understand what has been said. If, on the other hand, you didn't understand, your informational feedback gives him or her the opportunity to correct your impression.

That opportunity helps the other person continue to behave rationally and motivates him or her to stick with your conversation. You're still in control that way, even if (sometimes, especially if) he or she is doing all the talking. In a way, informational feedback strokes the other person's ego more effectively than does flattery. People like it when they know you're really listening to them, even if you don't understand them immediately.

Still, Charlie strokes Adam's ego more overtly. He says, "Since I know you to be a fair man . . ." That's not mere flattery. It reflects the image by which Adam wants to be known, and it helps Adam be fair. It's what is called *positive reinforcement,* and it's used only if it's sincere—only if the other person has done something for which he or she deserves to be rewarded. Charlie is rewarding Adam for backing away from his apparently inflexible attitude toward discussing a disagreement.

Once he has Adam moving forward, Charlie nails down that motivation for engaging in their discussion by offering several additional rewards. Then, he checks out just how successful he has been in negotiating this seeming impasse. As you saw, he now has Adam receptive and ready to hear his case.

Since you've already seen Charlie's case in support of a raise, I'll skip that portion of their conversation and get at the most important part of these negotiations—resolving the disagreement. I'll illustrate how to do that using as an example Adam's opinion that Charlie hasn't earned the respect of his people.

Charlie: I'm really surprised that you think my staff doesn't have respect for me. What makes you think that?

Adam: It just seems that they sass you a lot—give you a bad time about the work you assign them. I don't know what else, except it doesn't look good for employees to talk to their boss the way yours talk to you.

Charlie: Adam, I want to be sure I understand what you mean by respect. It seems to me you mean a civil tongue. Talking up to me rather than what you call "sassing." Is that right?

Adam: Yeah. That's what I mean. There's an awful lot of horseplay in your department—among the employees, too.

Charlie: Maybe that's where you and I disagree with regard to whether or not I'm too easy. We've already seen the figures—attendance, punctuality, error ratios, and the like. You've seen that my people always get their work done on time as well. Right?

Adam: That's right.

Charlie: How do those things relate to your interpretation of respect?

Adam: I guess what you're getting at is that if those people didn't respect you, they wouldn't do their work as well as they do. I think I see what you're saying.

Well, that's the easy one. Charlie pinned down what Adam meant by "respect," had him describe what he meant by "too easy." The upshot was that they disagreed on what constitutes "respect." Then, Charlie had only to get Adam to see for himself that respect also includes the type of performance he gets from his people. As I said, that's the easy one.

The difficult disagreement to resolve is the ultimate one—the raise and its amount.

Chapter 5

Getting Your Boss to Agree—Resolving Any Disagreements and Reaching a Consensus

Charlie has set the stage by making clear the purpose of the meeting. In fact, he had Adam's help in doing that because Adam knew perfectly well what Charlie meant when he had asked for a meeting in the privacy of Adam's office, a meeting to discuss the head bookkeeper's salary.

Our hero has kept the meeting moving forward toward his goal by appealing to Adam's needs and the company's goals as well as to his own. At each step along the way, Charlie has kept the issues focused on the merits of his work and on the quality of his leadership. He has let no emotional issues get in the way; he checked constantly to make sure the two men understood each other and that the feelings with which they had to deal never clouded the real issues.

And notice, Charlie never lets his own emotions get in his way. He has reason enough to be angry with Adam for not having been given a raise in five years, but he left those feelings outside the room. He knows enough about negotiating to recognize that the moment he loses his temper, he loses the whole ball game. Even if you win the battle, as the old saying goes, you lose the war.

Something else you've probably noticed. *Charlie never appeals to pity.* He never uses such arguments as: "But the cost of living has gone up. I can't make ends meet. My family's experiencing hardship." Those appeals will cost you the sympathetic understanding you want—they'll cost you the *empathy* you're trying to achieve.

Instead, Charlie keeps all emotional issues out of the discussion because he wants to demonstrate that his effort has contributed, in part, to the success of the company. He wants his raise to be Adam's recognition and reward for having made that contribution. He wants his share of the profits he has helped the company produce. That means focusing on the merits of the case and working through every disagreement until no further disagreements remain—until he and Adam reach consensus.

You've examined one disagreement and seen how Charlie controlled the discussion right through to its conclusion: achieving consensus as to what constitutes respect for a manager. The whole of this discussion has as its goal Charlie's raise. About this, reaching consensus won't be easy.

All this holds true for negotiating a promotion as well as a raise. Only the target of your objective is different. The preparation, the presentation, and the bargaining remain the same.

Let's return now to our story. Adam has accepted Charlie's interpretation of the quality of his work and leadership. It seems reasonable to conclude that Adam would also agree to a raise and to the amount for which Charlie is about to ask. Still, remember that Adam tends to guard the vault, and if he does nothing else well, he does guard that vault with the will of a dedicated sentry.

Adam: Charlie, I concede all that, but you're making $30,000 a year. That's more than any other manager in the company. As I said before, you've always seemed contented with that.

Charlie: Because I haven't asked for a raise before, I seemed satisfied with my salary.

Adam: That's right.

Charlie: I have to take responsibility for that. I should've spoken up earlier and didn't. No, Adam, I truly believe I'm worth a lot more than that.

Adam: From what I read, that's about what other head bookkeepers make.

Charlie: This analysis from the Department of Labor shows that many head bookkeepers with my education, training, and experience make $33,000.

	Some as much as $35,000. That's what I think I'm worth to the company, too.
Adam:	Thirty-five thousand dollars! That's one heck of a big jump in pay, Charlie.
Charlie:	You think that's too much.
Adam:	You're darned right I do.
Charlie:	O.K., what do you think's fair?
Adam:	Hold on. I haven't even agreed to a raise, yet.
Charlie:	O.K., then, Adam, what more evidence do you require to agree to it?
Adam:	[*After a moment's pause*] Charlie, you must be taking lessons from our salespeople. I've already agreed that you've done a great job here. I've agreed that I might've been wrong about how you manage your people. I'm feeling a bit trapped.
Charlie:	What does that mean?
Adam:	I'd sound foolish after all that to say, "No raise," but, Charlie, $5,000 would have a heck of an impact on your department's budget.
Charlie:	All at one time, it will. That's why I should've come to you sooner. It really amounts to only $1,000 a year that I should've been getting all along. At least that. That's why I asked you what you think's fair.
Adam:	If giving you that big a raise—giving you any raise at all—would have an adverse impact on your budget, how would that be fair to your people?
Charlie:	I don't understand.
Adam:	Wouldn't they see that as taking advantage of your position and padding your own wallet at their expense?
Charlie:	You think they'd be resentful.
Adam:	Sure. Wouldn't they be?
Charlie:	I don't think so. In fact, I think it'll have the opposite effect, because right now they believe that a raise for them is out of the question. None of them has received a raise since they've been here. Morale has been slipping. There's even a bit of grumbling going on down the hall. Now I think we can stop that growing discontent if we develop

	an amended budget that works to everyone's satisfaction.
Adam:	An amended budget?
Charlie:	It's something that I have in mind and that I know we can work out, if and when you agree to a raise. It'll prevent a whole lot of headaches later on.
Adam:	O.K. I'll concede the raise.

Cut! I'm stopping the action at this point because Charlie's reached objective No. 1: Adam has agreed to a raise.

Adam said that Charlie must be taking lessons from the salespeople because the bookkeeper's been doing what salespeople do when they manage the customer's objections. He's listened to what Adam has had to say. He's probed him for additional information, and he asked him to specify what more information Charlie has to present. He even used what salespeople call a trial close—"O.K., then, Adam, what do you think's fair?" He checked out whether or not Adam's ready to buy.

Of course, Adam called him on the trial close, but Charlie wasn't about to back down. He knew he had already received too many concessions from Adam to give up now. That's the purpose of checking out at each step of the presentation whether or not the other person agrees with you. As Adam said, since he had agreed to everything else, he'd "sound foolish after all that to say, 'No raise.' . . ."

Charlie not only listened and understood Adam's objections; he also dealt with them as they occurred. He has an answer ready for Adam in advance. As I said earlier, assessing your boss's attitudes requires that you consider what objections he or she might raise and prepare to answer them.

You'll recall that Adam considers himself to be a fair and rational manager. His self-image, in a way, had hoisted him by his own petard. He raised the "straw man" issue of fairness to the staff in bookkeeping. That gave Charlie the opening for stating how his raise will benefit the company—by paving the way for granting raises to other people as well. It would take some reassessment of priorities and some restructuring of the budget, but after all, that's one of the things for which a manager gets paid.

So, Adam concedes the raise. Now, Charlie has to bargain over the amount of that raise.

Adam: But $5,000 is out of the question.

Charlie: That's why I asked you what you think's fair.

Adam: [*After a moment's pause*] How about $1,000 this year and another thousand next year?

Charlie: You're offering $2,000 over a two-year period. Is that right?

Adam: Yes. That's right. I think that's fair.

Charlie: Because I haven't had a raise in five years, that would actually work out to $2,000 over a seven-year period. You agreed that I demonstrated my worth to your satisfaction. Unless I misunderstood, you agreed to that.

Adam: Sounds like you've got something else in mind, Charlie.

Charlie: O.K. For now, I'll settle for a $3,000 raise this year. That'll bring me in line with the going rate in my profession, and it'll compensate me to some extent for all that I've done for the company. How does $3,000 sit with you?

Adam: Except for the fact that it sounds as if you've got another shoe to drop, it sounds O.K.

Charlie: Then, you agree?

Adam: Yes—$3,000. Now, where's that other shoe?

Charlie: I've got something else in mind, that's true, but I want to say, first, that I appreciate your working this out with me. I feel a lot better about things. For the first time in a long while, I feel you appreciate my efforts. I want to thank you for giving me the consideration I think I'm due.

Adam: To tell the truth, Charlie, I'm glad you forced the issue. I hadn't given you enough credit. In fact, I've probably just taken you for granted. I pride myself on being fair, Charlie. You've given me a chance to put my money where my mouth is. Now, for Pete's sake, what else's on your mind?

Charlie: It goes back to that amended budget request. I think I can convince you of how we can absorb my raise and make provision for other raises in the department. Let me show you what I think we can do.

Negotiations over the raise have come to an end. Charlie achieved both of his objectives: getting a raise and getting the amount he believed from the outset would be realistic to expect. Though I compressed the conversation deliberately and had Charlie back off his initial request faster than most people should, achieving both objectives will come almost as easily as that if you are properly prepared; if you make a strong, factual, well-documented presentation; and if you resolve all disagreements as they arise.

Charlie's success was due, in part, to his ability to manage his boss's objections. Armed as well as he was, he moved Adam from "no raise" to "$5,000 is out of the question." From there he moved to "$2,000 over two years," and then on to a $3,000 raise this year. Well-armed and ready to bargain—that's the way to negotiate for a raise.

Haggling—The Fine Tradition of the Marketplace

Americans don't bargain well. We're used to walking into a store and paying the price marked on the ticket. We're used to accepting gratefully what's offered to us. I'll leave it to sociologists to try to explain why. For the purposes of this discussion, it's important that you realize you will have to haggle to get at least what you can expect rather than nothing at all or, at best, what someone else thinks you're worth.

Bargaining means nothing more than asking first for the highest raise or the biggest promotion you think the traffic might bear in order to leave room for retreating if, in fact, the traffic won't bear it. It means doing this and still coming away with something you want.

Charlie not only succeeded in getting most of what he wanted; he also gave Adam something in return: a boost for his ego and a way to prevent salary problems with other employees in Charlie's department. Both men got something out of the negotiations. That's why it's called a win-win strategy.

Charlie succeeded, but that doesn't give him grounds for gloating. In fact, gloating at this point would be self-defeating. Since he's already given Adam a chance to save face and preserve his image as a fair-minded boss, he can give Adam some appreciation for responding to Charlie's fair request. "Thanks." It's a simple word, but it opens the gate for additional discussions—and for another raise in the future.

Chapter 6

Additional Points About Asking for a Promotion

For the most part, if Charlie had been asking for a promotion instead of a raise, he'd have followed the same procedures. Still, consider a few additional points if you're looking to make a significant move in the company: What is the nature of the job you're after, how does it fit with your career plan, how well qualified for it are you, and who else wants it?

Factors to Consider in Planning Your Career

Remember when you were a kid and your mother used to say your eyes are bigger than your stomach? For a lot of people, the same can be said when they covet a particular job in the company. The authority is greater, the pay is higher, the prestige is more significant than what they have. In their eagerness, they forget to ask about the responsibility. That usually increases, too. Whether or not you want it, you have to decide if you can digest that big a portion.

That decision also depends upon whether or not the position really fits with your career plan. For the most part, when people think of a promotion, they think of going into management, even if they're quite good at and happy with what they're doing. Instead of working out career progressions that fit with their strengths, they move into other areas because it's "expected of them" or because it's "the way to get ahead." Frequently they wind up going nowhere. Sometimes they wind up going out the door.

The usual progression often leads to the so-called Peter principle—the idea of a person's being promoted out of the job in which he or she is most skilled into a position for which he or she has no training and/or experience. The position in which the person is incompetent is usually management. You can see how important it is for you to measure your own qualifications before taking a crack at a position that looks good on paper.

Recognizing that opportunities for upward movement in the company are limited (and the pyramids are now clogged at the top with relatively young people), many organizations are developing lateral career paths—creating senior technical positions or cross-training people to work in a variety of departments. They are then tying salary increases to performance standards or to a bonus system rather than to promotions. Before trying to climb to the next rung in your firm's management ladder, you might look into whether the firm offers other options.

Other options may become extremely important if you find that a promotion in your company depends upon skills you don't have. You could go out and get them by attending a school or training program, but by the time you're ready, the position you want may be filled. If you want to climb a particular ladder in your company, it's best that you make some serious plans early on for getting a leg up on the competition you're bound to meet along the way.

And the competition's going to be there. Unlike asking for a raise, in which situation many adjustments can be made to accommodate a number of people, only one person at a time can fill any given position. You can be sure that if you want that position, so do other people—not only your fellow workers but also all those outsiders who have heard of it.

Keep this in mind. In March 1985 a major airline, with over 30,000 employees, advertised in *The Wall Street Journal* for a staff manager. The firm received 175 responses to its *blind* ad. Can you imagine what the response would have been had the company revealed its identity?

If you wish to try for a promotion, be sure you know who your competitors are, their strengths as well as their weaknesses. You need to show that you know what the job entails, that it fits with the career plan you set for yourself a long time ago and for which you've prepared yourself, and that what you offer the company will benefit it more than if it promoted your most serious competitor.

Chapter 7

Now Is the Time for You to Act!

Negotiating a raise or promotion is just one form of negotiations—a situation in which two or more people have to reach an agreement in principle, or choose between alternatives, or take a specific action. Negotiation goes on constantly, not just in governmental relations or in labor-management disputes. You negotiate all the time with friends and relatives over a wide variety of everyday decisions.

You rarely take notice of most of your negotiations because they usually don't become obvious until some type of conflict arises, when your self-esteem and/or economic or physical well-being are at stake. When you want a raise, you recognize that all three conditions are threatened.

Decide on Your Goal

To minimize fear and frustration, and to give yourself a fighting chance at success, you have to recognize, first of all, that your economic destiny is really in your own hands. You have the power to get what you want, but you'll get it only if you develop the same strategy and tactics used by any negotiator.

You have to decide on exactly what goal you're trying to reach. What do you really want from these negotiations? A promotion? That's a given, but to what position?

A raise? That's a given also, but how much of a raise are you willing to accept? How much would you like to have, if you could get it, and how much can you realistically expect? Those are questions you have to answer first.

Select Your Strategy

Then you have to prepare yourself for making your case. You have to assess your position in light of labor-market and general market conditions. You have to assess the position of your organization and the position that your manager is bound to take.

Once you feel ready to move forward, you have to pick a negotiating strategy you think will work best under the circumstances. Most of the time, the win-win strategy of client-centered selling will work for anyone. By meeting each other's interests, if not by meeting commonly held interests, both parties come away with something. No one feels "the loser."

This strategy can be referred to as an assertive posture—one in which you can exercise your own personal power while at the same time not diminishing the other person's. You can obtain your rights without dominating or tyrannizing (threatening or blackmailing) him or her.

Some situations, granted, do call for an aggressive posture. You may have to dominate rather than control. You should be prepared to meet hostile strength with enough power to protect yourself in the clinches, but however and whenever you can, you should use your assertiveness rather than your aggressiveness. At the same time, when threatened with no raise at all, or when offered a pittance in return for meritorious duty, it's much more to your advantage to threaten to leave the company than to roll over and say, "Thank you."

Rarely, though, will you have to go on such an offensive if you have marshaled all your relevant facts; documented those facts; and made your presentation clearly, unambiguously, and forcefully. The best way to make a forceful presentation is to relate those facts to the benefits already received by the organization from what you've done and to what benefits will follow from granting the request. What's in it for them—that's what sells horseshoes to automakers.

Negotiate Effectively

How you negotiate also makes a difference. An assertive negotiator controls not through domination, but by using the proper mix of questions and assertions, by hearing out the other person first, and by explaining his or her position only after the other person's case is presented in its entirety. Then, and only then, can you work through the disagreements that arise between yourself and the boss.

Stating your case for the raise or promotion will cause other disagreements to surface as well. That's why you lead with your lesser points first, getting agreement on them before moving on to your major points. Listening to and responding to objections and resolving differences of opinion before proceeding will prevent them from creeping up again just when you think you're home free—and knocking you back to square one.

You have to get agreement on the merits of your work before you can get your boss to agree that you've earned a raise at all. And you have to get the boss to agree to that before you can get him or her to agree to the amount of that raise. Sometimes, you'll have to let the boss ventilate some emotions before you can get that agreement, too.

You have to get those emotions into the open when they appear to surface. Waiting until later could sabotage your whole effort. At the same time, you have to hold your own feelings in perfect check, avoiding at all cost any appeals to emotion. You might get your raise this time but find yourself out on the street if you pull too hard too often on the boss's heartstrings. He or she is running a business, not a welfare agency.

Finally, you have to remember that this is a win-win situation. The boss has to come away feeling good about the fact that he or she granted you the raise. There has to be something in it for him or her, too. You also have to express appreciation for whatever the boss has conceded (unless it comes to far less than could reasonably have been expected). Gloating at this point will make the next raise, if there ever is one, that much harder to get.

All that's left is for you to do what you know is right for you. You've earned your raise or promotion; you've got the documentation and have developed the case to back up your request. That's all you need to firm up the courage of your convictions. Go ahead and ask for what you want. There's nothing to stop you now.

Index

achievement résumé, 20,
 24–28
adjustment plan, cost-of-living,
 6
aggressive posture, 47–48
assertive posture, 47
awards, 28

bargaining
 haggling and, 43–44
 negotiations and, 16–17
 about salary, 42–43
belief, in oneself, 4–5
blackmail, 29, 47

career paths, 45
certificates, 28
checking-it-out technique, 35,
 41
client-centered sales, 31
 see also strategy, win-win
competition
 as ally, 9
 and negotiation, 15
 in promotions, 45–46
consensus, 38–43
 in win-win strategy, 31
contracts, *see* union contracts
cost-of-living adjustment plan, 6

critical-incident files
 certificates for, 28
 defined, 20
 job description for, 20–24
 résumé for, 20, 24–28

disagreements, 32
 negotiating, 34, 36–37, 38–43

emotions, 34–35, 38–39, 49
Equal Employment Opportunity
 (EEO), 10

Fair Labor Standards Act, 8
feedback, informational, 32, 36
feelings, *see* emotions
files, *see* critical-incident files
financial position, 13
 checking of, 13–14

goal setting
 importance of, 18–19, 47
 questions for, 19

haggling, 43–44
 see also bargaining
Hay system, 6
 bargaining in, 7–8

informational feedback, 32, 36
intangible assets, 27

job description, results-oriented,
  20–21
  creating, 22–24

Labor Department
  as reference source, 9
  on union contracts, 8
labor-market conditions
  checking of, 8, 9
  sources for, 9

market factors, 10–13
  checking of, 11
merit system, 8
mirroring, 34–35

negotiation
  bargaining and, 16–17
  defined, 15
  of disagreements, 34, 36–37,
    38–43
  effective, 48–49
  goal setting in, 18–19
  planning in, 17–18
  of promotions, 44–46
  techniques, 34–37
  versus competition, 15
  word selection in, 30
  see also strategy

opinions, 31–32

paraphrase, 35–36
performance-appraisal system,
  20
persuasiveness, 5
Peter principle, 45
pity, 38
  see also emotions

planning, 17–18
  questions for, 17
positive reinforcement, 36
power, 4
product-oriented companies, 12
promotions, 44–46

reputation, company, 27–28
results-oriented job description,
  20–21, 22–24
résumé, achievement, 20
  creating, 24–28

service-oriented companies, 12
strategy
  importance of, 29
  selection of, 47
  win-win, *see* strategy, win-win
  see also negotiation
strategy, win-win
  components of, 30–31
  example of, 39–44
  steps for, 31–34
supply and demand, 8

targets, 24–25
threats, 29, 47
timing
  determining, 14
  financial position and, 14
  importance of, 5–6
  market conditions and, 8–10
  market factors and, 10–13

union contracts, 6
  Labor Department statistics
    on, 8
  negotiation and, 6–7

Wall Street Journal, The, 46
win-win strategy, *see* strategy,
  win-win
word selection, 30

About the Author

Donald H. Weiss is an Account Executive for Psychological Associates, a training and development company, and President of Self-Management Associates, a small-business consulting firm located in Dallas. Along with the six books in the Successful Office Skills series, he has written numerous books, articles, video scripts, and study guides on business management and related topics. Dr. Weiss is the author of AMACOM's popular cassette/workbook programs *Getting Results, How to Manage for Higher Productivity,* and *Managing Conflict.*

Dr. Weiss holds a Ph.D. in social theory from Tulane University, as well as degrees from the University of Arizona and the University of Missouri. He has also taught at several colleges and universities. He is a member of the American Society for Training and Development.